AMERICAN HISTORY BY DECADE

The
1910s

Titles in the American History by Decade series are:

The 1900s
The 1910s
The 1920s
The 1930s
The 1940s
The 1950s
The 1960s
The 1970s
The 1980s
The 1990s

AMERICAN HISTORY BY DECADE

The
1910s

Deanne Durrett

KIDHAVEN
PRESS™

THOMSON

━━━━━━ ✦ ━━━━━━
™

GALE

San Diego • Detroit • New York • San Francisco • Cleveland
New Haven, Conn. • Waterville, Maine • London • Munich

© 2004 by KidHaven Press. KidHaven Press is an imprint of The Gale Group, Inc., a division of Thomson Learning, Inc.

KidHaven™ and Thomson Learning™ are trademarks used herein under license.

For more information, contact
KidHaven Press
27500 Drake Rd.
Farmington Hills, MI 48331-3535
Or you can visit our Internet site at http://www.gale.com

LIBRARY OF CONGRESS CATALOGING-IN-PUBLICATION DATA

Durrett, Deanne, 1940–
  The 1910s / by Deanne Durrett.
    p. cm. — (American History by Decade)
Summary: Discusses the 1910s including music, dance, women's suffrage, movies, and World War I.
Includes bibliographical references and index.
  ISBN 0-7377-1746-7 (hardback : alk. paper)
1. United States—History—1909–1913—Juvenile literature. 2. United States—History—1913–1921—Juvenile literature. 3. Nineteen tens—Juvenile literature. [1. United States—History—1909–1913. 2. United States—History—1913–1921. 3. Nineteen tens.] I. Title. II. Series.
  E761.D87 2004
  973.91'3--dc21
                                                                              2003010069

Printed in the United States of America

Contents

CHAPTER ONE

American Song and Dance

In the 1910s no one listened to the radio, and television had not been invented. No one had a cassette player or a CD player. And no one had earphones. When people wanted to hear music, they went to see live musicians. Today new songs are played on the radio or television. In the 1910s new songs were introduced in the local theater, called vaudeville.

In the 1910s songwriters wrote songs about flying machines, the automobile, courtship, the war, political campaigns, and issues of the day such as women's right to vote. Popular music of the time had simple tunes and easy harmonies that most people could sing. And a piano player needed only about a year's worth of lessons to play most songs. When people heard a song they liked, they wanted to enjoy it at home also.

Home Entertainment

Instead of buying records for home entertainment, people bought sheet music. Sheet music contained the words to sing and music to be played—usually on a piano. And most families had a piano in their parlor.

Playing the piano was a desirable social skill. Children in wealthier families took music lessons from a local piano teacher. Some people, however, were self-taught. Many people wanted to play an instrument to entertain family and friends. As a favorite pastime families and friends gathered around the piano and sang.

Barbershop Quartets

People also enjoyed singing and listening to barbershop quartets. These singers sang in four-part harmony. Each male quartet included a tenor, lead, baritone, and bass. They gathered four at a time in the local barbershop or on a street corner. One singer blew the beginning note on a

Sources: Bureau of Labor Statistics; Kingwood College Library; *National Vital Statistics Reports*, vol. 51, no. 3; U.S. Census Bureau.

Then and Now

	1910	2000
U.S. population:	92,407,000	281,421,906
Life expectancy:	Female: 51.8 Male: 48.4	Female: 79.5 Male: 74.1
Average yearly salary:	$750	$35,305
Unemployment rate:	2.3%	5%

small instrument called a **pitch pipe**. All four singers hummed in harmony together and with the pitch pipe note. Then they began to sing without a musical instrument.

The 1910s were part of the golden age of barbershop music. The barbershop songs of this decade included "Let Me Call You Sweetheart" (published in 1910), "If You Were the Only Girl in the World" (1916), and "Darktown Strutters

Children gather around a piano to sing. Many families in the 1910s had a piano.

Ball" (1917). The quartets sang older songs along with new ones.

American music had many influences. Some popular tunes came from before the Civil War on southern plantations in the slave quarters and the cotton fields.

African American Influence

After the Civil War, some freed slaves started developing a musical style that was based on the negro spiritual that they had sung on the plantations. This music told of their feelings and the hard times they had seen. Each musician blended his or her song of sorrow and joy with the others. A new music developed from these jam "sessions."

Some of these black musicians found work in New Orleans, Louisiana, night spots. From New Orleans, they brought this new music up the Mississippi River as riverboat entertainers. This music became known as ragtime and blues. Ragtime was a happy piano rhythm, and the blues sound often came from a horn with words that told of personal heartache.

Black musician Scott Joplin played ragtime piano and composed music in the 1910s. Although the first black entertainers began singing and playing to white audiences in this decade, Scott Joplin remained best known in the black community. His music, however, influenced white songwriters, including Irving Berlin. One of Berlin's hits of this decade, "Alexander's Ragtime Band," was similar to Joplin's music. (In fact, some people thought it was Joplin's music.) This was one of the ways black music became more acceptable to whites.

In 1914 blues found its way to mainstream America with the publication of "Saint Louis Blues," written by W.C. Handy. This piece was popular with both black and

This reproduction of a sheet music cover features Irving Berlin's hit "Alexander's Ragtime Band."

white audiences. Handy wrote in his autobiography that the sound of the blues was born in his mind when he was a boy in school and "the song of a Negro plowman half a mile away fell on my ears."[1] As a result of this incident, Handy wrote music from the heart based on deep feeling.

Handy directed a concert at the Metropolitan Opera in Atlanta, Georgia, in which the audience was mostly white. When the band played the "Memphis Blues," the audience wanted to hear the song nine more times. Handy wrote that, for the rest of the performance, they "played only requests, and these called for blues, blues, and more blues."[2] "Saint Louis Blues" became a hit in Europe as well as America. Today this classic is still enjoyed all over the world.

The Fox-Trot

Another way that people enjoyed music was ballroom dancing. In fact, some people call the 1910s the ballroom decade. People danced the waltz and tango to orchestra music. Of course, the orchestras played the latest hits, including ragtime and blues.

These new rhythms called for a new dance. Most people think this dance, the fox-trot, was invented by vaudeville star Harry Fox. As part of his act, Fox began doing trotting steps to ragtime music. Before long other dancers were "trotting" to ragtime. This dance is a pattern of slow, slow, quick, quick steps that can be danced in place on a crowded dance floor. The popularity of the fox-trot spread to Europe along with ragtime and blues.

Tin Pan Alley

People listened to music. They danced to it. And they made music themselves. For this to happen someone had to write it, publish it, and put it in the hands of the people. Tin Pan Alley did this.

The term "Tin Pan Alley" was first used as a nickname for a street in New York City that was lined with music publishing companies. By the 1910s, however, the entire music publishing business was called Tin Pan Alley. From its beginning in the late 1800s until it became less important in the 1950s, Tin Pan Alley created America's music.

The music publishers hired music composers and lyricists to write the music to be published as sheet music. Some of it was written on demand for professional entertainers. However, all the sheet music was marketed to the general

Ballroom dancing was a very popular form of entertainment in the 1910s.

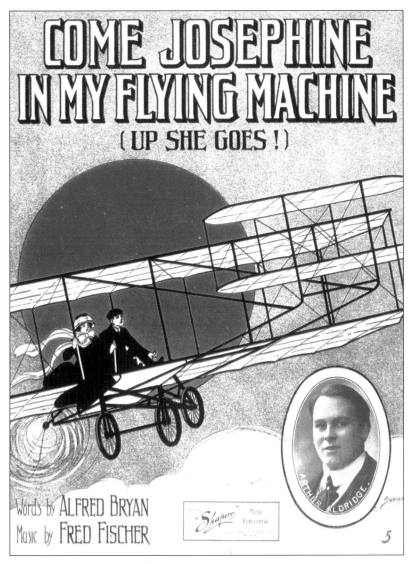

Tin Pan Alley published the sheet music for the most popular songs of the day.

public. Over the span of several decades, the greatest American composers of all time wrote music printed by Tin Pan Alley. These included Irvin Berlin, George M. Cohan, Scott Joplin, and John Philip Sousa. Although Tin Pan Alley is gone, the music published by it is still enjoyed today.

CHAPTER TWO

Women Fight for the Vote

In 1912 women had the right to vote in nine states only. These were the western states of Wyoming, Utah, Colorado, Idaho, Washington, California, Oregon, Kansas, and Arizona. In some of the other thirty-nine states, women could vote in some local elections, usually school-board elections. **Opposition** to full women's **suffrage**, however, (allowing women to vote in local, state, and federal elections) remained strong in these states.

Women Divided

Many women, as well as men, opposed the vote for women. These women and men believed that men were more knowledgeable, less emotional, and should be the decision makers. Wives followed their husband's thinking. In fact, the laws said that a woman was her husband's possession, and she had little say about her own life. When she married she lost her personal identity and rights to her possessions and future children. This was the way things were. Many woman accepted this and did not think the vote for women mattered much.

Women who supported women's suffrage wanted a different life for themselves and all women. Before women got the vote, they were second-class citizens with few rights.

A woman was expected to marry and spend her life raising children. For this reason formal education for girls was not considered important. Only girls from wealthy families received higher education. A few of them went to college to become professionals such as doctors and lawyers. Most, however, went to finishing school where they

Many men of the 1910s thought women should not have the right to vote.

learned the proper way to pour tea, housekeeping methods, manners, and how to play an instrument and entertain guests.

There were few career opportunities for women besides being a teacher or nurse. Uneducated women from poorer families who needed to work usually took in laundry or worked in factories for lower wages than men. Life was very hard for an uneducated woman without a man.

A woman usually went directly from her father's control to her husband's. A man made all the decisions and had all the rights. He owned the property. He controlled the money. A wife was expected to bear children. It was common for a man to divorce a wife who could not have children.

Most women, however, had little choice but to stay married. Laws protected a husband's property rights, even when the husband spent all the money gambling and drinking and let the family go hungry. A woman was not likely to leave. She had nowhere to go and no reasonable way to support her children. If divorced or left by her husband, any wife could find herself facing serious hardship.

Women desperately needed a better way of life. They needed to have the same legal rights as men. They needed someone in government to speak for their needs. For this to happen women needed to win the right to vote.

Joining Forces

The Women's Christian Temperance Union also wanted a better life for women. This group focused on men who wasted the family income on alcohol and gambling. When some men drank too much they made life difficult for their wives and children. Members of the temperance union believed that women would vote for candidates who would write laws to outlaw liquor. These women joined the suffrage movement and began working to win the vote for women.

Other groups also saw that women would vote for candidates who supported their cause. These groups included people who wanted better working conditions, fair wages, better housing for the poor, and an end to child labor. These people joined in the campaign for women's suffrage. In fact, the suffrage movement was made up of several groups, each group with its own leader.

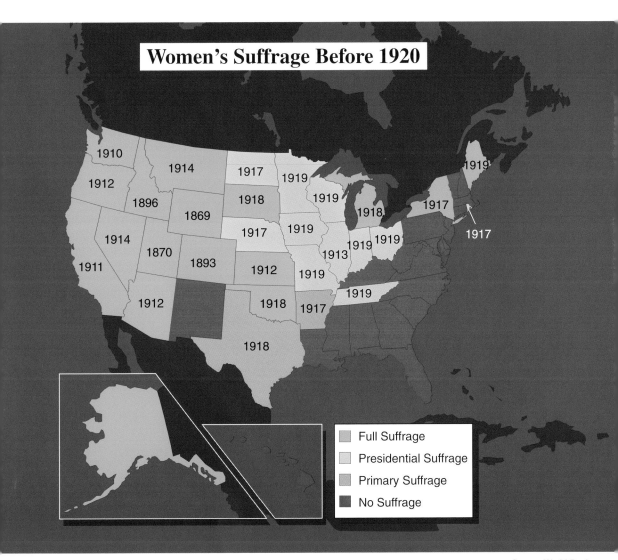

Women's Suffrage Before 1920

Full Suffrage
Presidential Suffrage
Primary Suffrage
No Suffrage

Source: World Book.

WHICH NEEDS IT MOST?

SALOON KEEPER — PAY ENVELOPE — **HOME MAKER**

For the Money Represented by

Three Ten Cent Drinks

a Day For a Year

Any Grocer in Your Town Will Give You the Following Groceries:

15 Fifty-pound Sacks of Flour	50 Cans Tomatoes
20 Bushels Potatoes	10 Dozen Oranges
100 Pounds Granulated Sugar	20 Dozen Bananas
10 Pounds Salt	50 Cans Corn
50 Pounds Butter	25 Pounds Beans
20 Pounds Rice	100 Cakes Soap
50 Pounds Oat Flakes	1 Pound Pepper
25 Pounds Coffee	4 Gallons Molasses
5 Pounds Tea	20 Gallons Oil

And There Would Be ENOUGH MONEY LEFT To Buy a Good Present For Your Wife and Babies

The Women's Christian Temperance Union produced posters like this one to discourage men from wasting money on alcohol.

Suffrage Strength Fades

Leaders such as Elizabeth Cady Stanton, Lucretia Coffin Mott, and Susan B. Anthony dedicated their lives to gaining the vote for women. Unfortunately none of them lived to see the victory. They had all died by 1906. The loss of these leaders left the movement stalled until the beginning of the next decade.

New Leaders and New Tactics

In the 1910s, however, strong leaders arose who carried the suffrage movement to victory by the end of the decade. The new leaders included Harriet Stanton Blatch and Carrie Chapman Catt.

The new leaders followed in the footsteps of the founders of the movement. Harriet Stanton Blatch was Elizabeth Cady Stanton's daughter. Susan B. Anthony chose Carrie Chapman Catt as her **successor**.

Carrie Chapman Catt unveiled her "winning plan" in 1916. Her plan was to work for suffrage at the state and federal levels at the same time. In other words, some **suffragists** continued working to win the vote in the remaining states. At the same time others would take the battle to Washington, D.C., and work for a constitutional amendment.

In addition, Catt and other leaders adopted aggressive tactics used by suffragists in England. This included protests, hunger strikes, and marches.

The First March

The first march took place in New York City in 1910. Dressed in white dresses with skirts to their ankles and collars buttoned at the throat, the ladies wore hats, gloves, and high heels that clicked in unison as they marched. They wore "Votes for Women"[3] pennants angled across their chests. Some marchers carried large signs demanding the right to

Suffrage movement leader Carrie Chapman Catt marches in New

vote. Working-class and middle-class women united for the cause in these marches. The marchers impressed the audience with their growing number, attitude, and strong will.

Suffragists held many other marches. They held a march and pageant on April 13, 1913, the eve of President Woodrow Wilson's inauguration. During the pageant Florence Noyes dressed in an elaborate Miss Liberty costume. (Miss Liberty represented liberty for women.) The march and pageant were held in protest of Wilson's refusal to support votes for women.

Suffragists held many marches to spread their message.

The battle for the vote continued throughout the decade with even more aggressive tactics. And the opposition, also, grew more aggressive. Marchers were attacked. Some were arrested. Some suffragists were jailed. Some went on hunger strikes. They also tried to get state and federal legislators on their side. They wrote articles and delivered speeches. Using all these tactics they attempted to convince men in high office, as well as male voters, that women should have the vote.

Victory at Last

The Nineteenth Amendment passed the U.S. Senate on June 4, 1919. Obtaining **ratification** by the required thirty-six states took another fourteen months of hard work. Tennessee became the thirty-sixth state to ratify, and women officially gained the constitutional right to vote on August 18, 1920. The victory gave women a voice in the government and opened the door to gain equal rights. In decades to come, women would continue to fight battles to gain education, career opportunities, and better pay.

CHAPTER THREE

Silent Film Comes to Vaudeville

Silent films (the first movies) made their debut on the vaudeville stage. They were short films usually four to five minutes long and shown between live variety acts in a vaudeville show. The audience loved the novelty of photoplays, as they were first called. People flocked to the theater to see a film of anything moving. This included a baby crying, trolley cars on the move, or even a tree with branches blowing in the wind. In fact, the first movie, made in 1893, *Fred Ott's Sneeze*, was a close-up of a man sneezing.

By 1910 moviemakers had learned to make movies that were long enough to tell a story. People liked these even better.

The Moviemakers

Film studios were located in New York state, Chicago, and California. California had the best weather, and the west provided good scenery. As a result Hollywood soon became the movie capital of the world. Some of the early studios that made silent films are still making movies today. These include Warner Brothers, Metro-Goldwyn-Mayer (MGM), Fox, and Universal.

A director stands near the camera on the set of an early silent movie.

Hollywood produced hundreds of films a year, and large audiences of people enjoyed them all. Longer films became the main show, and these silent movies moved to their own theaters.

Movie Theaters

On a typical evening in the mid-1910s, about 5 million Americans "went to the show"[4] (movie show). By this time there were twenty thousand movie theaters in the United States. Many of these moviegoers lived in small towns and attended local movie houses. Big cities, however, had large, fancy theaters called palaces. These theaters seated from twenty-five hundred to six thousand people. Movie historian Ben Hall said that a movie palace was "an acre of seats in a garden of dreams."[5] Large cities such as New York and Chicago had several glamorous palaces where **patrons** received royal treatment, including beautiful lounges for men and women, smoking rooms, nurseries, and refreshments during intermission.

The Sound of Silence

The films of this decade did not have sound. Still, the actors communicated with the audience very well. They clearly mouthed the words and expressed themselves expertly with body language and hand gestures. Where additional information was needed, printed words appeared on the screen between scenes.

By 1913 small movie houses had pianos and large palaces had orchestras that played along with the film. Some composers wrote special music to set the mood for certain scenes. The musicians watched the film and played music suitable for the action on the screen. The music ranged from fast and furious to calm and peaceful. Some music brought sad feelings, while other music made the audience feel happy.

Actors in silent films used body language, facial expressions, and hand gestures to communicate with the audience.

The Stars

Silent films offered something for every taste, including drama, comedy, action, and romance. The stars of the 1910s such as Mary Pickford, Charlie Chaplin, and Douglas Fairbanks were best known for a specific type of movie.

Mary Pickford was known for drama. She became one of the most popular movie stars of all time. She reached the peak of her career in 1917. Her most famous movies include *The Poor Little Rich Girl*, *Stella Maris*, and *Daddy Long Legs*. In the 1910s Mary Pickford was known as "America's Sweetheart."

Silent film star Mary Pickford is one of the most popular actresses of all time.

Douglas Fairbanks made his way from vaudeville to the movie screen. He made his first movie in 1915. By the end of the decade he became known for his roles as a swashbuckler. Fairbanks was best known for his roles as a skilled swordsman who won all his battles in action-packed movies.

Another silent film star, Charlie Chaplin, came to the United States from England in 1910. He made his U.S. film debut in 1914. By 1915 he had created the clown character that would make him world famous—Charlie, a baggy-pants bum known as The Little Tramp. In 1916 Chaplin was the highest paid actor in the world, with a salary of ten thousand dollars a week.

Actor Douglas Fairbanks (right) was best known for his roles as a skilled swordsman.

Charlie Chaplin became famous for his role as The Little Tramp.
In 1916 he was the highest paid actor in the world.

The Perils of Pauline, one of the most famous serial movies in history, starred Pearl White (center).

Serial Movies

During the 1910s, serial movies drew Americans to movie theaters week after week. These short films, usually about twenty-five minutes long, were shown before the main feature. Each episode ended with a cliff-hanger, and moviegoers came the next week to see what happened next. A number of series were released in the 1910s, including *The Perils of Pauline* (1914), *Mystery of the Double Cross* (1917),

The Master Mystery (1918), *Lightning Bryce* (1919), and *Woman in Grey* (1919).

Film historians recognize *The Perils of Pauline* as one of the most famous suspense serials in cinema history. The twenty-episode thriller starred Pearl White. As one of the most remembered episodes ends, Pauline is tied across the railroad tracks and a train is roaring toward her. Pearl White made 195 movies from 1910 to 1919. She is best remembered, however, as the heroine in *The Perils of Pauline* series.

The silent film era lasted into the 1920s. It ended when Hollywood began making talking pictures. Modern technology, however, has made it possible for people today to enjoy the silent films of yesterday on television movie channels.

The Great War

As World War I began in Europe in 1914, U.S. president Woodrow Wilson declared that America would remain neutral and stay out of the conflict. The United States continued trade with Germany as well as European countries who were enemies of Germany. America's neutrality changed, however, when German U-boats (submarines) began sinking merchant ships with American citizens and American cargo on board.

The United States Enters the War

The U.S. Congress declared war on Germany on April 6, 1917. People did not have radios or televisions in their homes then. So most people read that the United States had entered the war in newspaper headlines. As soon as they received the news, many young American men volunteered to fight in the Great War, as it was called then. The United States, however, did not have the huge number of troops it needed to send to France.

Selective Service

When there were not enough volunteers, Congress passed the Selective Service Act. The act required men between twenty-one and thirty-one years of age to register for the

draft. A year later still more troops were needed, and the draft age was expanded to include men aged eighteen through forty-five.

Doughboys

American men from all walks of life answered the call to serve. Nicknamed doughboys, they came from farms and cities. Some were well known and others would make a

American men who were drafted to fight in World War I were called doughboys.

name for themselves in history. For example, Harry Truman (future president of the United States) commanded an **artillery battery** on the western front. Doughboy Hollywood celebrities included Buster Keaton, a silent film star. He later stated that his service in the Great War was "an experience I have never forgotten."[6]

Food Crisis

American fighting men needed food. And the doughboys could not expect to find it waiting for them when they arrived in France. German U-boats had been sinking cargo ships in the Atlantic Ocean. Tons of food being shipped to Europe had been lost. As a result of the war and this loss, the Allied countries were facing famine conditions.

President Wilson asked the American people to help. He called for patriotism and sacrifices—he asked Americans to grow more food and eat less.

Food for the Troops

Within a week of the president's request, a plan was in place for everyone to avoid eating wheat on Mondays, meat on Tuesdays, and pork on Saturdays. Housewives and school children signed pledge cards promising that they would eat everything they put on their plates at meals and avoid snacks between meals. Americans were encouraged to eat more corn, oats, and rye cereals and breads. They were also encouraged to eat fish, poultry, fruits, vegetables, and avoid fried foods. The idea was to save wheat, red meat, sugar, and fats to feed the U.S. troops and Allies.

People planted gardens in every suitable place, even in vacant lots that did not belong to them. They ate leftovers and did not waste food.

To encourage this patriotism the government had posters designed and printed to display indoors and outside.

The government printed posters like this one to encourage
Americans to help increase the local food supply.

One of the posters, for example, read, "Food is ammunition—Don't waste it." Another read, "Be patriotic. Sign your country's pledge to save the food."

War Bonds

Other posters encouraged people to do other things to help the war effort. For example, the government issued **Liberty Bonds** and encouraged people to buy them.

Bonds are actually loans that are paid back with interest after a few years. Posters advertising the bonds were posted everywhere. And famous movie stars toured the United States on Liberty Trains, encouraging people to buy bonds. Mary Pickford, Charlie Chaplin, Douglas Fairbanks, and many other stars went on tour for Liberty Bonds. Most stars promoted the bonds, and almost everyone gave money to the war effort. Instead of giving money, some people volunteered their time and skills.

Volunteers

The American Red Cross organized a volunteer force. Some people went to France to care for the wounded. These included nurses and ambulance drivers. They cared for the French people as well as the troops.

Other people contributed by working at home. They rolled bandages, sewed hospital garments, made surgical dressings, and knitted socks. American people also helped the people of France and Belgium who lost their homes. Volunteers made clothing for babies. They packed comfort bags that contained safety pins, soap, a washcloth, talcum powder, six needles, white thread, and a thimble. The whole nation joined the battle when Americans went to fight World War I.

The American military force that went to France was called the American **Expeditionary** Force. By the time

Posters like this one urged people to buy bonds to help the war effort.

American Red Cross workers and Boy Scouts display donations collected in Alabama. Some Americans donated money while others donated their time and skills to the war effort.

American troops arrived in France, the western front stretched through France from the North Sea to the Swiss border. Along this line Allied and German forces faced each other from trenches on either side of no-man's-land.

German trenches were on high ground while the Allied trenches were on low ground. Groundwater seeped into Allied trenches and made life miserable. Some doughboys stayed in these muddy trenches for as long as three weeks in wet clothing. During these times their feet swelled in their boots and hurt so badly they could not walk.

Riflemen and machine gunners fought from the trenches while heavy artillery guns positioned well behind the line lobbed shells overhead into enemy territory. Neither side advanced more than a few miles.

The biggest threat to Allied troops in the trenches came from poison gas. This was the first time poison gas had been used as a weapon. The Germans released chlorine and mustard gas and let the wind carry it to Allied trenches. At first

An Allied soldier eats while seated in a trench. Life in the trenches was miserable.

A soldier and his horse wear gas masks as protection against poison gas.

the Allies did not know what it was. They saw a cloud of green gas floating from the German line toward them. When it arrived Allied troops began to suffer and die. The Allied forces fashioned protective hoods to wear during gas attacks.

Dogfights and Aces

German and Allied troops fought World War I in the skies as well as the trenches along the western front.

Each side flew **biplanes** equipped with machine guns on missions behind the other's line. The pilots observed enemy artillery sites and troop movements. Of course, neither side wanted these locations revealed. When pilots took to the air, they expected to meet the enemy in the sky.

The battle between aircraft was a deadly game of tag called a dogfight. The biplanes were easy to fly, and each pilot did aerial acrobatics to avoid being hit by the other's machine-gun fire. At the same time each pilot tried to gain a position in the sun behind the enemy plane. This position would make him invisible to the enemy pilot and give him the opportunity to aim his machine gun on the back of the enemy pilot's seat. The dogfight usually lasted until one plane fell to the earth in flames. The victorious pilot wanted credit for his kill (victory). An American pilot became an ace once he had five confirmed kills.

Although American pilots came into the war late, they helped the Allies win the victory.

The Great War was said to be "the war to end all wars." It was not. Still, 1910–1919 was an impressive decade filled with accomplishments that would benefit the world.

Notes

Chapter One: American Song and Dance

1. W.C. Handy, *Father of the Blues: An Autobiography*. New York: Da Capo, 1941 (renewed by heirs 1969), p. 137.

2. Handy, *Father of the Blues*, p. 128.

Chapter Two: Women Fight for the Vote

3. American Press Association (photo), *Suffrage Parade*, New York City, May 6, 1912. Library of Congress. http://memory.loc.gov.

Chapter Three: Silent Film Comes to Vaudeville

4. "Some Enchanted Evenings: American Picture Palaces," American Studies at the University of Virginia, June 20, 2002. http://xroads.virginia.edu/~CAP/PALACE/.

5. Quoted in John Margolies and Emily Gwathmey, *Ticket to Paradise: American Movie Theaters and How We Had Fun*. Boston: Bulfinch, 1991, p. 14.

Chapter Four: The Great War

6. Quoted in Martha R. Jett, "My Career at the Rear: Buster Keaton in World War I," Doughboy Center: The Story of the American Expeditionary Forces, September 2000. www.worldwar1.com/dbc/buster.htm.

Glossary

artillery battery: The military group whose duty is to operate artillery, large guns with a range of several miles.

biplane: An early airplane with two sets of wings, one above the other.

draft: Required military service.

expeditionary: Troops sent on an expedition to another country to fight.

Liberty Bonds: Savings bonds the U.S. government sold to the public to support World War I.

opposition: The other side.

patrons: Customers, usually at a theater or restaurant.

pitch pipe: A small whistle used by singers to establish a note on which to begin singing.

ratification: A state's vote to approve an amendment.

successor: One who serves in office next.

suffrage: The right to vote.

suffragists: People, mostly women, who favored women's right to vote.

For Further Exploration

Books

Simon Adams and Andy Crawford, *Eyewitness: World War I*. New York: DK, 2001. This book is an overview of World War I that includes pictures and illustrations.

Beth Seidel Levine, *When Christmas Comes Again*. New York: Scholastic, 2002. This "Dear America" historical fiction is an account of an Army Signal Corps volunteer and offers a good view of life overseas during World War I.

Carol Rust Nash, *The Fight for Women's Right to Vote in American History*. Berkeley Heights, NJ: Enslow, 1998. This book gives an overall account of the fight for women's suffrage with information about the leaders of the movement.

Ruth Turk, *Charlie Chaplin: Genius of the Silent Screen*. Minneapolis: 1999. An action- and information-packed biography of Charlie Chaplin, The Little Tramp.

Websites

Historic American Sheet Music (http://scriptorium.lib.duke.edu/sheetmusic/timeline-1910.html). This website features sheet music covers of the 1910s. With a click of the mouse, the music can be viewed page by page—notes and words.

Ohio State—Woman Suffrage (http://1912.history.ohio-state.edu/suffrage). This page offers an overview of the issue with opposing viewpoints plus a look at some political cartoons of the time.

The Works of John Philip Sousa (www.dws.org/sousa/works.htm). This website offers audio examples of John Philip Sousa's marches, many of them written in the 1910s.

Index

Picture Credits

About the Author

Deanne Durrett is the author of nonfiction books for children from third grade to high school. She writes on many subjects and finds research and learning exciting. Durrett now lives in a retirement resort community in Arizona with her husband, Dan. Other members of the household include Einstein (a miniature schnauzer dog) and Willie (an Abyssinian cat). You can visit Durrett's website at www.deannedurrett.com.